Born in 1977, the author spent the first few years of his life living in his father's ancestral village, St Abbs, Berwickshire, Scotland. The family then moved to Shetland where he spent the majority of his childhood, before settling in Arbroath for the remainder of his teenage years. He now lives and works in Dundee with his wife and three young children.

This book is dedicated to the life of Dave Gibson (1950–2017), life-long socialist, trade unionist and anti-racist activist, who passed away before his research on our ancestor, Isabel Cowe, came to fruition.

Iain. E. Brown

ISABEL COWE: SHORE GULL AND SUFFRAGIST

THE PROVOST OF ST ABBS

AUSTIN MACAULEY PUBLISHERS™

LONDON • CAMBRIDGE • NEW YORK • SHARJAH

A CIP catalogue record for this title is available from the British Library.

ISBN 9781528987585 (Paperback)
ISBN 9781528987592 (ePub e-book)

www.austinmacauley.com

First Published (2021)
Austin Macauley Publishers Ltd
25 Canada Square
Canary Wharf
London
E14 5LQ

I would like to thank Geoff Gibson, Noreen Thompson (Gibson), Zoe Lovell, Jo Ladd, Kate Burland-Gibson, Effie Aitchison, Mum and Dad, Bobby Kerr at the Luckenbooth (Coldingham), wife Debbie Brown and grandparents Jim and June Nicolson (née Gibson), without whom none of this would have been possible.

Table of Contents

Coldingham Shore

The small fishing village of St Abbs is located 20 miles south of Dunbar on the east coast of Scotland, and was originally named Coldingham Shore.

The Shore fishermen were initially housed at Fisher Brae in Coldingham, with a fair sized community also present at Northfield. However, in the mid-18th century that all changed when the first house was built in the village, on the site of the present Rock House.

In the latter part of the 18th century, five houses were constructed in a row, at what was to become the Under Row (Harbour terrace). By the 1830s, the Under Row had expanded considerably, with houses being built by fishing families such as the Raes, Wilsons, Cormacks and the Thorburns.

The fisher folk of Coldingham Shore have always used a special term of endearment for one another, which continues to this day. The term 'Shore Gull' is used to identify anyone born or brought up in the village.

Birth (Under Row)

Born at 10 in Under Row, on the 1st of December 1867. Isabel Cowe was the youngest of eight children of Robert Cowe and Catherine Rae. Her parents were both children of fishermen from Eyemouth and Coldingham.

Having been steeped in the traditions of the fisher-folk, their way of life was passed down through the generations, and they knew no other working environment other than the sea.

The way of life was very hard for these fishing communities, and whilst the men were away at sea for weeks on end, the women and children were ashore, working to gut and preserve the fish, bait lines and repair nets. In the evening, mothers would be found at the spinning wheel, telling the children tales of witches, fairies and hobgoblins, as well as songs, poems and traditional Scottish folk stories.

Coldingham Shore – Under Row in 1868 now Harbour Terrace, St Abbs

Education

Up until 1872, when the Education (Scotland) Act was introduced, a child's education consisted largely of learning the trade of their parents, unless they were fortunate or wealthy enough to do otherwise.

The Act made it compulsory for children between the ages of 5 and 13 to attend full-time education. This was to have a big impact on the lives of the fisher-folk. On one hand, many working class families struggled to adapt to this change, as they relied heavily on all members of the family being involved in the industry, whilst others were happy for their children to be given a chance to make something for themselves and improve their quality of life.

Isabel began her schooling at St Abbs Hall, which was initially used as a school until 1887. She was one of the first of a generation to be given the opportunity to broaden their horizons, and to dream of a world outside of the small fishing village in which generations of her family had lived and worked together.

The demand for schoolteachers across Scotland was on the rise due to the introduction of the new Education (Scotland) Act. In 1875, my great great grandfather Alexander Gibson left his birthplace of Closeburn in

Dumfriesshire. He arrived in Coldingham Shore, where he took up the position of schoolmaster.

He was soon to become Isabel Cowe's brother-in-law, when he would marry her elder sister Euphemia Cowe on the 6th of November 1877.

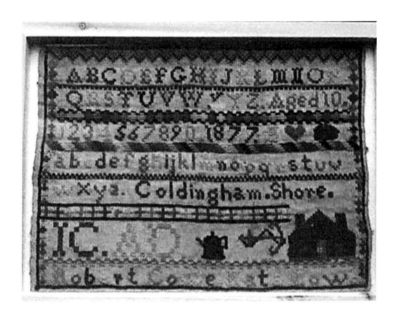

A cross-stitch by Isobel Cowe

Family Tragedy

The way of life for the fishermen of St Abbs and the fishing industry in general had always been wrought with danger, and the life-threatening working environment they experienced on a daily basis meant the loss of life was never far from home. And this was always foremost in their minds.

On the 31st March 1879, the family was to experience such a loss, when Isabel's elder brother Robert Rae Cowe was lost at sea aged 26. This was a terrible loss for the family, and for Isabel, at the tender age of twelve, her first experience of grief. However, there was a far greater tragedy to come for the family, and the wider fishing community of the east coast.

Black Friday (Disaster Day)

The great storm of the 14th October 1881, known locally as 'Black Friday' or 'Disaster Day', left 107 widows and 351 fatherless children within the east coast fishing communities of Eyemouth, Burnmouth, Cove, Fisher-Row, Coldingham Shore and Newhaven. It was Scotland's worse ever fishing disaster with the loss of 189 men.

Isabel was only 13 years old when the entire male working population was wiped out and decimated, leaving the women and children of these communities destitute, and extremely fearful of the future.

Her uncles Andrew Cowe and John Cowe were both lost on that fateful day. Andrew was on the boat 'Industry' leaving nine children fatherless, whilst John was on the boat 'Fiery Cross' leaving behind a pregnant wife and seven fatherless children. This sent shockwaves through the Cowe family, and with sixteen of Isabel's cousins left fatherless, she looked on in horror, as her whole family were thrust into a life of grief, pain and suffering on an unimaginable scale. These fishing communities had always been used to the sporadic loss of life, and were used to dealing with such situations. But the grand scale of the Black Friday disaster was unheard of, and this new territory proved very hard to bear.

It was suggested that many of the fatherless children be given places in the Quarries Children Home, but the local mothers refused, saying, "We shall keep our bairns for the future of our ports."

This statement alone speaks volumes about the women of these communities: it is the single mindedness, tenacity and determination of these women that left a legacy for thriving communities to be proud of their heritage.

In the aftermath of the disaster, Isabel witnessed first-hand how capable the women in her family and community were. They had no option but to stand on their own two feet and support their young families. They rose to the challenge with great strength, determination and resilience, for the love of their community and their way of life.

As the women rallied together, Isabel began observing many extraordinary acts of selflessness, learning many valuable lessons for the future, lessons in overcoming adversity, resilience, tenacity, compassion and in never giving up the fight for what is right; most importantly, the lesson of how capable women were, in a time when they were regarded as second best to men.

St Abbs Black Friday memorial sculpture

Census 1881

In the 1881 Census, Isabel is residing at Beach House, Coldingham Shore, with her sister, Euphemia, and brother in law, Schoolmaster Alexander Gibson. She is described during this time as his sister-in-law and a scholar. Isabel would have most certainly received an above average education whilst living in the same household as her schoolmaster brother-in-law, with this regarded as a great privilege in those days.

In the years between 1881 and 1900, we don't have too much information about Isabel. However, in an article from the Berwickshire News, we find reference to Miss Cowe, having been known as a singer in her younger days, and having local fame as a raconteur of Scottish stories.

Isabel's talent of storytelling was most probably developed and passed down from within the fishing community, where it was commonplace for mothers and elder siblings to tell stories and folk tales to the children.

This talent brought her in contact with Marjory Kennedy Fraser, the famous singer and reciter of Hebridean folk songs. The two women remained lifelong friends, until their last meeting at St Abbs Haven in August 1930.

The Usher Family – The Birth of St Abbs

The year 1885 saw the arrival of Andrew Usher, the successful Scottish whisky distiller to Coldingham Shore. Mr Usher played a major role in the improvement and regeneration of the village, and his philanthropy changed the lives of everyone in the community.

Usher funded the new village hall and school, the extension of the harbour and the building of the new church. He fought to get a fresh water supply for every home, and electric lighting for the village hall. However, this came with a stipulation which still stands to this day: the opening of a public house was prohibited in the village.

In the 1890s, Mr Usher put forward a proposal to change the name of the village from Coldingham Shore to St Abbs. His proposal was accepted.

Usher's presence increased the profile of the village, and began attracting many new and wealthy visitors and holidaymakers. Isabel Cowe's brother-in-law, the Schoolmaster Alexander Gibson, who was also the secretary and treasurer of the harbour trust, was in direct contact with Mr Usher during the regeneration process of the village. Therefore, we can be certain that his wife Euphemia, sister of

Isabel, would have been keeping her family informed of all the plans Mr Usher was making regarding the village.

Laird Andrew Usher

John Usher (brother of Andrew)

The Bicycle – New Women of the 1890s

Another of Isabel's passions was cycling, and in the book 'Ebb Tide' by Will Wilson, a native of St Abbs and proud Shore Gull, we find reference to her cycling from John o' Groats to Land's End, which at a distance of 875 miles is still regarded as the holy grail of distance cycling. This is no easy undertaking and would have taken at least two weeks to accomplish.

The 1890s brought about the peak of the bicycle in the UK, Europe and America, and it is said that 'the bicycle had done more to emancipate women than anything else in the world.'

Women like Isabel seized the bicycle as a tool of personal and political power, which was prevalent in these new women of the 1890s. The 'New Women' was a feminist ideal that emerged in the late 19th century, and was used to describe the growth in the number of feminist, educated and independent career women in Europe and the United States.

The 'New Women' pushed the limits set by a male-dominated society, and from this small seaside village of St Abbs on the Berwickshire coast, Isabel Cowe began gravitating towards becoming one of these independent 'New Women'.

Census 1891

In the 1891 Census, Isabel, aged 23, is registered as living with her parents at 7 Brierylaw, St Abbs, which was later renamed 'The Anchorage'. Her father Robert Cowe is recorded as a retired fisherman, aged 63 years, and her mother Catherine Cowe is recorded as his wife, aged 65 years.

Isabel Cowe with her parents

Isabel's sister, Agnes Cowe, is absent from the records during this period as it seems she spent time in an asylum. In fact, we have records of a six-month spell in the 1890s.

Death of Parents

Isabel, who is now the only child living at home, would spend the next six years dedicated to caring for her ageing parents.

Sadly, in 1895, her father dies aged 67. Then in 1897, her beloved mother passes away, aged 71.

The Anchorage

Following the death of their parents, the family home at 7 Brierylaw was passed onto Isabel and her sister, Agnes. This is supported by the 1901 Census, which lists both women as summer lodge keepers, at the Anchorage, St Abbs.

The sisters seem to have found a new purpose in life, and following Laird Andrew Usher's decision to regenerate the village, as well as the rise of the phenomenon that was the British seaside holiday, they settled into this newly found role, which broke the mould of the conventional role society gave women. The sisters were now involved in the pioneering role of seaside landladies and female business owners, in a time before the vote was given to women.

This was a huge turning point in Isabel's life, despite still dealing with her sister's continual mental health problems, which must have been very challenging.

In 1905, Isabel is listed as the proprietrix of the Anchorage Lodging house, St Abbs.

Front view, Anchorage, St Abbs

Miss Jane Hay

This same year saw the arrival of Miss Jane Hay, the pioneering feminist and internationally renowned humanitarian campaigner to Coldingham.

The 'St Abbs Haven' was originally built as Miss Hay's home and office, when due to ill health she was advised to move to more tranquil surroundings. The remainder of her life was spent helping orphans and local children go onto better things, and improving the lives of those less fortunate than herself.

Jane Hay found a kindred spirit in Isabel Cowe, a woman who possessed natural feminist ideals and qualities, shaped by her upbringing and life experiences. Armed with Miss Hay's knowledge of the wider political world, they joined forces to enlighten others, in the ideologies of the new women of the 1890s.

Miss Hay enjoyed the company of many creative and intellectual people involved in the feminist cause. And both women shared a friend in common, Singer Marjory Kennedy Fraser.

The famous Dymock poet and writer, Wilfrid Wilson Gibson, and his older sister, Elizabeth Gibson, visited St Abbs Haven often. Wilfrid Gibson's play 'Womankind' with its message of female solidarity was popular amongst suffragettes in the UK and US. In 1914, his dramatic poems 'Mates' and 'Summer Dawn' were reprinted in Sylvia Pankhurst's socialist feminist paper, 'The Women's Dreadnought', having first appeared in his book 'Daily Bread', which was dedicated to 'J.H., St Abbs Haven'.

Below is an extract from a letter Wilfrid Gibson wrote to a friend, author and poet, Dorothy Una Ratcliffe (Brotherton):

"In my youth, I spent many months at St Abbs Head, at the home of an old friend, Jane Hay. It has been the source of quite a number of my poems. It was in that house I met a man who had gone to Flannan Island, to find out the cause of the lighthouse not working. The first lighthouse I ever explored was the St Abbs one, to gain inspiration for my poem, the Flannan Island Lighthouse."

Gibson then goes onto say that his early poems about the fisher folk were suggested to him at St Abbs by a friend of Miss Hay, who was of fisher stock herself. He must have been referring to Isabel Cowe, who we know was a reciter of poetry in her younger days.

Wilfrid's sister, Elizabeth Gibson, was actively involved with the Women's Social and Political Union and the National Union of Women's Suffrage Societies, along with Jane Hay, who chaired a WSPU meeting in Berwick, the special guest at this meeting was Adela Pankhurst.

There's no doubt St Abbs Haven would have been a hive of activity and conversation relating to women's suffrage, and I'm sure many important women connected with the cause would have visited Miss Hay on a regular basis.

Author & Poet, Wilfrid Gibson

Author & Poet, Elizabeth Gibson

Marjory Kennedy Fraser

Jane hay (1864 – 1914)

Women's Freedom League (WFL)

In 1907, the Women's Freedom League (WFL) was created by 77 members of the WSPU, who disagreed with Christabel Pankhurst's announcement to cancel the WSPU annual conference. The organisation was founded by the romantic novelist and social reformer Charlotte Despard, and was created to promote civil disobedience rather than physical violence or property damage.

Isabel Cowe was a member of the WFL and we know this due to her involvement as one of the organisers, and prime movers, in the 1912 Edinburgh to London Suffrage March, which was funded by the WFL. The WFL was a more democratic organisation than the WSPU, they refused to attack people or property other than the ballot papers, unlike the WSPU. Therefore, we can be certain that Isabel Cowe was a suffragist, as appose to a suffragette.

The Alfred Erlandsen

On the 17th October 1907 at 20:00 pm, the two-masted Danish steam ship 'S.S Alfred Erlandson' whilst on route from Riga to Grangemouth struck the rocks of Ebb Carrs reef, just off St Abbs.

Because of the fog, the first people of St Abbs knew about the disaster was the sounding of the ship's horn and the vessel grating against the rocks. The Eyemouth and Skateraw (Dunbar) lifeboats were called out to assist, but due to the severity of the conditions, all 18 hands were lost.

Following the tragedy, Miss Jane Hay of the St Abbs Haven wrote to the Edinburgh Evening News on the matter, "As one of those who witnessed the tragedy, I shall never rest content till we have a lifeboat and rocket apparatus of our own at St Abbs."

Miss Isabel Cowe and Miss Jane Hay spent the next four years campaigning to secure a lifeboat for St Abbs.

Loss of Another Brother

In 1908, during the campaign for a new lifeboat, Isabel is again faced with a death in the family when her elder brother, James Cowe, is lost at sea, aged 57 years.

St Abbs' Lifeboat – The Helen Smitton

On 25th April 1911, the St Abbs' lifeboat, The Helen Smitton, was commissioned and launched, and a lifeboat station opened.

Miss Cowe was a member of the Lifeboat Committee of Management since its inception, and given her love and commitment to the RNLI and the lifeboat crew, we can be certain that she was part of this campaign.

It has been documented that the Usher brewery family of Northfield House were the main financial contributors of the lifeboat.

St Abbs' lifeboat The Helen Smitton

Four Tonnes of
Railway Sleepers

In the 1911 Census, Isabel, by this time 43 years old, was still listed as a boarding housekeeper of the Anchorage, which is recorded as having nine bedrooms. It was one of the most popular boarding houses in the area during the season, and Isabel, with her kind and genial nature, was especially well known amongst the summer visitors.

She was always keen to make sure the best interests of the village and community were being honoured, and was always happy to take up matters with the local parish council.

One such occasion was when the parish council refused to act after the community complained, via Isabel, about the state of the roads and coastal paths. Isabel took it upon herself to order four tonnes of railway sleepers, costing £26, and had the roads put in order. The creel road to Coldingham, footpath to the sands, and the footpaths leading to the harbour. In order to pay this debt back, Isabel had to organise concerts, from which she raised £16. The other £10 was raised by other means, such as tea parties, picnics and home baking sales.

To put this cost into perspective, in 1905, the yearly value of her boarding house 'the Anchorage' was £19.

Isabel Cowe was the type of person who would get things done, for the good of her community, then deal with the financial side later.

It was through acts like this which earned Isabel the title 'The Provost of St Abbs' from the local people who had come to know and respect her.

S.S. Glanmire

The year 1912 would prove to be one of Miss Cowe's most eventful years.

On the 25th of July 1912 at 06:20 am, the iron steamship, S.S. Glanmire, while en-route from Amsterdam to Grangemouth, in thick fog, struck Black Carr's rock, then drifted off to sink 300 metres north of St Abbs' lighthouse, about half an hour later.

In the 30 minutes it took for the Dundee built ship to sink, Miss Cowe gave assistance to the fishermen who went out in two boats to rescue the 15 passengers and 22 crewmembers, giving them all shelter and hospitality at the Anchorage.

If it hadn't been for the quick response, and actions of Miss Cowe and the fishermen of St Abbs, all 37 souls would have perished that morning.

RNLIs – Golden Brooch Award

Miss Cowe had a warm spot in her heart for the lifeboat men, and never wearied working for their cause. She organised many functions to raise funds, including fancy dress parades in the summer, when she herself led the procession in colourful fishwives' costumes or sea captain uniforms.

The outstanding charitable work which she carried out for this noble cause received tangible recognition, in the presentation of the Royal National Lifeboat Institutions Golden Brooch, and a record of thanks in vellum.

They also made her an honorary member of the institution in recognition of the valuable services rendered, an honour which she deeply appreciated and of which she was justifiably proud.

Golden Brooch Award

Charitable Organisations

Isabel Cowe not only worked tirelessly for the RNLI and the St Abbs' lifeboat crew, she also donated and was involved with other organisations such as the Edinburgh Royal Infirmary, the local nursing association, and the Children's League of Pity.

This charity work brought her recognition, not only from within her local community but much further afield in areas across Scotland.

The Fairy Godmother and the
Provost of St Abbs

A great lover of children, each year she gave a Christmas treat and a summer picnic to the young people of St Abbs and district, the children regarding her as a fairy godmother. At the Christmas celebrations of 1930, they presented her with a lovely rose bowl in grateful recognition of her many acts of kindness to them.

Happiest when helping others, she organised numerous concerts and fancy dress parades in the village during the holiday season, making her a favourite with holidaymakers and children alike.

A popular figure in the village, with her kind and genial nature, she quickly endeared herself to her many visitors, and fighting the parish council for the rights of her beloved St Abbs earned her the title of 'The Provost of St Abbs'.

Even now her many deeds of kindness are recalled and her memory, although faded, will be remembered in years to come.

Votes for Women – Edinburgh to London March

In October 1912, Isabel Cowe was to help organise and participate in the gruelling 400-mile Scottish Suffrage March from Edinburgh to London. The aim was to procure signatures en-route, before carrying a Votes for Women petition to the prime minister, H.H. Asquith.

The march set off from Edinburgh on the 12th of October 1912 and arrived in London on Saturday the 16th of November, taking over four weeks to complete. It followed the great north road through Berwick, Belford, Alnwick, and Morpeth.

Initially, 300 women began the march in Edinburgh, on a wintery October morning, headed by Miss Charlotte Despard and Miss de Fonblanque, and supported by thousands of spectators and a brass band who gave them a fantastic send off. However, after the first few miles in awful weather, the numbers dropped dramatically. In the exposed winter conditions, many onlookers were in admiration of the brave marcher's enthusiasm and determination.

The Brown women, as they were known, in their brown coats, brown felt hats with green cockades, white scarfs, and heavy footgear, could be seen marching up to fifteen miles per day, attending organised meetings and events at each place they stopped.

We find reference to Miss Cowe in the Berwickshire Journal being described as an enthusiastic recruit. She was asked, "How the women are standing the strain of the long march?"

She replied with a homely illustration, "It's like this, when I begin spring cleaning after the winter rest, I feel very stiff, and the first day especially is a hard grind, but afterwards get used to it and don't feel it, these ladies will find the great walk like that, and a day or two will put them in thorough training."

Miss Cowe, who joined the marchers at Dunbar on her bicycle, had done some splendid work en-route, with the bicycle enabling her to reach many out of the way farm places and hamlets for signatures, before re-joining the main group.

Her experience of wrecks and storms at St Abbs had made her hardy and helpful, and even in the roughest weather during the long march, she never missed a chance of getting a signature. Wearing a Sou'wester, and holding a hurricane lamp and pen and ink, she made a picturesque figure. Furthermore, she would ride ahead of the main group, to secure lodgings at every intended location.

Berwick-upon-Tweed

The women reached Berwick on the 16th of October, following a 30-mile stage of the march from Dunbar, in torrential rain.

Mrs Le Fonblanque addressed the crowd in Berwick, and remarked that they had not felt the cold despite the weather because "The fire of enthusiasm burns within us, and we are carrying the torch of light."

The women left Berwick the following day in bright sunshine cheered by the number of signatures they had obtained.

The following year, the Northern Men's Federation for Women's Suffrage was founded and a branch formed in Berwick.

A newspaper clipping

Suffragists crossing Berwick bridge.

The Bluebell Inn – Belford

Belford inhabitants turned out in great numbers to greet the marchers. This support had been expected from the town, which in 1792 had submitted a petition against the slave trade, notable for the large number of women who signed it.

In the Belford and District museum, we find photographic evidence of the suffrage march. A photographic glass plate shows suffragists outside the Bluebell Inn; clearly visible among the group of women outside the hotel is a suffragist holding a bicycle. Undoubtedly, this is Isabel Cowe (age 44).

In the same picture are four suffragists holding a large 'Votes for Women' banner. A horse and carriage, which contained the petition for the prime minister, and the marchers equipment was also present. The horse, named Butterfly, was a mare belonging to organiser, Miss Le Fonblanque. Bred and broken in by her, the horse completed the whole journey.

Suffragists at the Bluebell Inn

Belford, Isabel Cowe on bicycle

Suffragists at the Bluebell Inn

Suffragists at the Bluebell Inn

Morpeth

The group reached Morpeth on Saturday the 19th of October at around 17:00 pm.

In the evening, they held a meeting in the market place, where a very large and orderly crowd assembled. The speakers for the ladies expressed themselves as well pleased with their reception throughout the country. They were keen that the public should know that there would be no militancy on the march, which was of a peaceful manner.

The petition was presented to sympathisers at the close of the meeting.

The ladies remained in private lodgings in Morpeth for two nights, before setting off for Newcastle on Monday the 21st of October.

Newcastle

On arrival in Newcastle, a grand demonstration took place and a special church service was held.

Local organiser, Laura Ainsworth, headed the welcome party at the Blue House, North Road. They marched down Northumberland Street, Pilgrim Street, Hood Street and Grey Street taking tea at the Turks Head.

Newcastle became the first city council to pass a resolution to grant suffrage to women in 1913, an action which was the brainchild of Laura Ainsworth.

Trafalgar Square, London

The marchers arrived in London on Saturday the 16th of November, meeting four to five thousand sympathisers at Camden Tube Station, before being escorted to Trafalgar Square. Miss Cowe was named as one of six who had covered the whole distance.

The brave Brown Women swung into Trafalgar Square to the tune of 'See the Conquering Heroes Come' and 'March of the Women'. They met with a very cordial reception on reaching Trafalgar Square, where a considerable crowd of people awaited them. Three platform meetings were held, at which a resolution praying that the government would bring in a bill, giving votes for women this session.

The Petition – H.H. Asquith

By the time the petition reached London, it boasted thousands of names and signatures with the plea, 'We the undersigned, pray the government to bring in a bill for Women's suffrage this session.'

In the afternoon, Mrs Florence Gertrude de Fonblanque, the organiser of the march, and Miss Margaret Byham proceeded to 10 Downing Street, where they presented the petition to one of the prime minister's secretaries, who promised to lay the document before Mr Asquith.

Sadly, but as expected, the petition had little effect on Mr Asquith. However, the march and the petition had promoted the cause in new areas and reached parts of the country like North Northumberland, where the movement had barely penetrated up until then.

The Edinburgh to London march of 1912 was a precursor for the Great Pilgrimage of 1913. It inspired and influenced many suffragist organisations, giving them strength and determination to push ahead with a bigger, better organised march, which would reach out to a far greater number of people across the country.

Westminster Abbey – Sunday Morning Service

On Sunday the 17th of November, Isabel and twenty suffragists attended the morning service at Westminster Abbey. They were dressed in their distinctive Brown Women marching uniforms, and must have made an impressive sight.

In the afternoon, they held a public demonstration in Hyde Park, which unfortunately failed to attract the numbers of the public they had intended.

Silver Medal

The six original marchers were each presented with a silver medal for their participation and completion of the march.

Egham to Land's End

It appears that Isabel remained in London after the march to continue her support for the cause. This is verified from a newspaper article from the Egham area of London.

The article states that Isabel Cowe, of St Ebbes, was riding her bicycle on a footpath on December 12th 1912 at 10:45 am on London Road, Egham.

A police officer, PC Hoare, stopped Isabel who replied, "I thought I was doing no harm?" And that 'she asked a man if she could ride on the path and he said it was okay to do so!' She told the officer 'she was a suffragette on her way to Land's End.' Miss Cowe was fined 5/-.

A short animation of this incident was made by children of Egham in 2017.

SUFFRAGETTE AND POLICEMAN.

At Chertsey Sessions on Wednesday, Isabel Cowe, of St. Abbe's, Berwick, was summoned for riding a bicycle on the footpath at Egham on Dec. 12th. Defendant did not appear, and P.C. Hoare said at 10.45 in the morning he was in London Road, Egham, and stopped defendant when riding on the footpath. Defendant said she thought she was doing no harm. The road was in fair condition.—Asked her age, the constable hesitated and then replied "I should say 45. (Laughter). She said she was a Suffragette, and was one of those who had walked from Edinburgh. She was riding to Land's End when I stopped her." (Laughter). Defendant told him she asked a man if she could ride on the path, and was told "yes."—Find 5/-.

Throughout the Country

Isabel Cowe and thousands of likeminded folk throughout the country were bravely beavering away; both militant and constitutional activists, each with their own stories of injustice to tell, and coming together as a collective force in the hope of facilitating this monumental political change.

London may have been the centre of the most dramatic events during the long campaign for women's votes, but from Shetland in the north to the Channel Islands in the south, and from Ireland to East Anglia, societies of busy men and women agitated their communities to join the crusade.

A Deputation of Working Women – January 1913

In January 1913, the WSPU organised for a deputation of working women to appear before the Chancellor of the Exchequer, David Lloyd George, to present a very strong case for women's suffrage.

Women had been at the heart of the manufacturing powerhouse during the empire since the industrial revolution. They frequently outnumbered men in factories, in the coalfields, workshops, schools and hospitals, yet because they lacked political influence, in most cases, their hours were longer and their pay lower. This was fundamentally unjust.

The Great Pilgrimage – 1913

The Great Pilgrimage was a six-week protest march, undertaken from 18th of June – 26th of July 1913, by thousands of suffragists or non-militant supporters of Votes for Women. It was arguably the single most influential event in the fight for the vote. Unlike the suffragettes, the suffragist organisations considered the fight for the vote to be a spiritual campaign.

The pilgrims were asked to be non-threatening, disciplined and dignified at all times during the march, so that people wouldn't confuse them with the often violent and militant suffragettes.

The march began with a meeting at Carlisle followed by meetings at forty towns en-route to London.

Isabel Cowe placed an advertisement in the Suffragette newspaper on the 13th of June 1913, offering accommodation to suffrage marchers at her boarding house, 'The Anchorage in St Abbs'.

Refusing to Pay Her Parish Rates

In the Berwickshire News of January 27th 1914, we find an article in which debt collectors have attended her home 'The Anchorage' to remove and sell goods. This was in light of Miss Cowe's refusal to go to Coldingham to pay her parish rates.

It was her zeal for the reputation of St Abbs as a holiday resort which brought her into conflict with the local authorities, over an alleged nuisance caused by a refuse depot at Murrayfield, St Abbs. The refuse was not being collected on a regular basis, causing a very bad odour in the area. Miss Cowe had heard many complaints and was concerned that this may have a detrimental effect on the number of visitors and holidaymakers coming to the village, and in turn, her business. The parish council said they could not improve the sanitary arrangement until St Abbs was formed as a scavenging district, which meant extra taxation for each household, for the service.

Miss Cowe argued that she knew of an agreement which allowed Northfield House to receive a regular collection, and she knew of other companies willing to collect the refuse, without extra taxation. However, the council still wouldn't change their position on the matter.

Miss Cowe then asked the collector of the rates to come to St Abbs, as there were over 70 households, but he took no notice. He sent Leslie & Leslie Debt Collectors. And whilst Isabel paid her rates, she refused to pay their expenses.

The sale of Miss Cowe's goods to cover the expenses took place on Saturday the 24th of January 1914. A standoff ensued involving Miss Cowe armed with a fire extinguisher and an axe, refusing to allow them entry. However, they eventually resolved the matter peacefully, gained entry and removed goods.

Miss Cowe told the Parish council the households in the rest of the village would be withholding their rates next year, which had the desired effect, because the following year the collector did indeed come to St Abbs!

Death of Jane Hay

On the 26th of January 1914, Isabel was to learn of the sudden death of her friend and kindred spirit, Miss Jane Hay of St Abbs Haven. Miss Hay's death occurred at Monnetier-Mornex, near the Swiss frontier of France. Her body was brought back by sea to Leith, of which she was a native, and thence home to St Abbs Haven, before being buried at Coldingham churchyard.

Her funeral took place on Saturday 31st of January and was attended by a great company of people from this country and abroad, many of national importance, but many more numbered among those of humbler stock, each with their own individual reasons to be grateful to her.

Miss Cowe, who was one of the only women in the district permitted to attend funerals, attended the funeral with Mr Mcallum, the St Abbs' schoolmaster, as well as schoolteacher Miss Munro and all of the pupils.

Marjory Kennedy Fraser was also present, paying her respects to a dear friend.

Adoptees of Jane Hay

The three youngest adoptees were taken in by Miss Octavia gillies Thomson, at the Rest, St Abbs, where they lived for 3–4 years. They then relocated to Edinburgh until Miss Thomson's health became very poor, she eventually moved back to St Abbs where she lived with Miss Cowe at The Haven.

Jane Hay at The Haven

The Haven

On the death of Miss Hay, The Haven was bought by Miss Cowe and turned into a boarding house/hotel.

On the coloured stained glass door at the main entrance, there is a painting of the fishing boat 'Kate Cowe', which was named after Isabel's mother. The boat, in full sail, is pictured leaving St Abbs harbour on her maiden voyage to Stornoway, and below are the words, 'And he bringeth them unto their desired Haven.'

The St Abbs Haven was one of the most popular boarding houses in the area, mainly due to the kind and genial nature, and reputation of the owner and hostess, Miss Isabel Cowe. The prominent coastal position and outstanding viewpoint was also a great selling point for holidaymakers. Visitors would return year on year; some were fourth generation visitors. Isabel insisted that everyone who came to The Haven had to kiss her!

The Haven could accommodate 100 guests in its prime, with Miss Cowe retiring to an outhouse when the hotel was full, the roof of this humble abode being formed by an upturned boat.

They kept their own cows, poultry and garden produce, which meant the highest quality meals were provided for all guests.

Kate Cowe fishing boat stainglass window

Stainglass window at The Haven hotel

Services Offered at The Haven

Miss Cowe provided weekly, daily and weekend accommodation, with guests paying on a weekly basis if staying multiple weeks.

She offered breakfast, dinner, afternoon tea and supper, with room service also available. Guests could enjoy either a hot or cold bath, with hot water bottles and fires available in every room – all at an extra cost.

Electric lights and wireless radio were available, with tennis or a walk around the lovely gardens on offer for more adventurous guests.

Miss Cowe managed to secure a licence to sell alcohol, which was the first to be issued in the St Abbs parish. However, to this day, there are still no licensed premises in St Abbs.

Grace – Every Day for 34 Years

When news of the First World War came to St Abbs Haven Hotel, there was a silent company for supper that night. Then suddenly, Miss Cowe, the proprietrix, spoke from her place at the table. "If you'll allow me," she said, "I'd like to lead you in singing grace." Everyone in the room sang the lines:

"Let us with a gladsome mind, Praise the lord for he is kind,

For his mercies aye endure, Ever faithful, ever sure."

From that day, the grace became a regular part of life in the hotel with Miss Cowe leading; it was sung before breakfast, lunch and supper.

When Miss Cowe died in 1931, her nephew, Mr David Gibson, took over the business. Every day, he led the grace, until 1941 when he moved to Portpatrick.

H.M.S. Pathfinder

Even in the tranquillity of small coastal villages like St Abbs, the horrors of war were never far away.

On the 5th of September 1914, Miss Cowe witnessed the H.M.S Pathfinder being torpedoed by a German U-boat off St Abbs' head. It was the first ship to be sunk using a motor-powered torpedo, causing the death of 250 people. The tragedy is verified in a postcard Isabel sent to a friend, Mrs Lothian of Edinburgh. The postcard is still in the possession of a relative today.

Interestingly, we also find an account of this incident by famous British writer Aldous Huxley, in a letter written to his father. Aldous and his brother Julian, who were staying at Northfield House, witnessed this devastating incident whilst enjoying a coastal walk.

"I dare say Julian told you that we actually saw the pathfinder explosion – a great white cloud with its foot in the sea."

"The St Abbs' lifeboat came in with the most appalling accounts of the scene. There was not a piece of wood, they said, big enough to float a man – and over acres the sea was covered with fragments – human and otherwise. They brought back a sailors cap with half a man's head inside it. The explosion must have been frightful."

In the few days following the incident, body parts continued to be washed ashore at St Abbs and Coldingham, which was very distressing for the locals.

The Pathfinder disaster had such an effect on Admiral Sir John Jellicoe that he decided to keep his grand fleet as far north as the Admiralty would allow.

The Haven and a postcard about the Pathfinder incident.

Aldous Huxley, witness of Pathfinder incident.

Julian Huxley, brother of Aldous

The First World War and Women's Suffrage

The First World War brought an end to activism in the suffrage cause, much to the delight of Prime Minister H.H. Asquith, who had taken no steps towards granting women the vote, despite the dedication and actions taken by numerous suffrage organisations during his reign.

However, 'Millicent Fawcett' held the NUWSS together by directing its 50,000 members into war work, gaining admiration by a wide range of male politicians for her efforts.

Women not only worked as nurses but began driving ambulances, running the railways and working in factories. David Lloyd George, the first senior politician who occupied the newly created post of minister of munitions, a job he held from 1915–1916, also joined the cause. He was so successful at motivating the female workforce and increasing production of shells for the battlefield that he raised his profile and the morale of all female workers. This led to his rise to prime minister in December 1916.

It must be noted that before the war, under PM Asquith, only men over 21 years who owned property had the right to vote. However, in 1917, Lloyd George granted the vote to all servicemen. The elevation of Lloyd George to the top job encouraged the suffragists to restore the campaign for Votes for Women. His respect for women and their contribution during the war effort led to a Royal Assent being given to the representation of the People Act 1918, which allowed women over the age of 30 the right to vote, providing they were householders, the wives of householders, occupiers of property with an annual rent of £5 or more, or graduates of British Universities.

On the 6th of February 1918, Isabel Cowe became one of 8.5 million women in the UK who qualified to vote; this was due to her being 50 years old and a property/business owner.

On the 14th of December 1918, Isabel Cowe cast her first vote. It was to be the first step towards full citizenship for all women, a goal which was finally achieved in 1928.

New Year's Celebration at The Haven

On the 14th of January 1930, the Berwickshire News reports how Miss Cowe entertained the St Abbs' lifeboat crew and 150 local folk. The New Year's celebration took place on Saturday the 11th of January at The Haven.

The Rev Nicholson proposed a toast to, "Our Hostess, Miss Cowe," he then remarked upon the generosity of Miss Cowe, "her loyalty and devoted interest to the cause of the lifeboat and also her many acts of kindness to the village and the inhabitants."

Instrumental music, singing and dancing was organised, with her relative Joe Gibson having travelled from his home in New Zealand entertaining the crowd with his spectacular playing of the mouth organ.

Marjory Kennedy Fraser

In the August of 1930, Marjory Kennedy Fraser visits Isabel at The Haven and they enjoy a good catch up, even though both women are in a very poor state of health.

Sadly, on the 22nd of November 1930, aged 73, Marjory Fraser dies in Edinburgh, and is buried on the Isle of Iona.

Isabel attends her funeral, even though her own health is deteriorating.

Majrory Kennedy Fraser

Miss Cowe – Death

In late November 1930, following the start of building work at The Haven, in the form of a new extension, Miss Cowe becomes seriously ill with a suspected heart attack and is bedridden.

She writes to her nephew, Robert Mortimer, in Australia following her heart attack and expresses her hopes for the future.

By mid-December, she makes a slight improvement and is again able to walk around, being seen occasionally in the village. However, at the end of December, her illness reoccurs and she is again bedridden.

On Saturday 3rd of January 1931, Miss Isabel Cowe passes away peacefully, aged 64.

The Funeral

On Tuesday the 6th of January 1931, a very large congregation, including the school children, accompanied by their teachers, attended the funeral service of Miss Isabella Cowe of St Abbs Haven, which was held in St Abbs church at 1 pm.

The coffin, covered with wreaths, was carried into the church by members of the St Abbs lifeboat, in their lifeboat attire.

The congregation sang 'Nearer, my God, to Thee', which was one of Miss Cowe's favourite hymns.

In accordance with a request by Miss Cowe before she died, her remains were cremated at Edinburgh Crematorium, and on Wednesday, in the presence of her numerous relatives, a private service was held, when her ashes were scattered on the lawn in front of The Haven by her cousin Mr Robert Cowe of Eyemouth.

Scattering of Isabels ashes at The Haven

Easter Service – Unveiling of the Sundial Memorial

On Sunday the 5th of April 1931, a memorial to the late Miss Isabel Cowe was unveiled at the St Abbs Haven.

The memorial was funded by over 215 subscriptions from the length and breadth of the country, by the many people who came to know and respect her.

The organisers of the appeal received numerous suggestions, and after very careful consideration decided that the memorial should take the form of:

1) A framed photographic enlargement in sepia of Miss Cowe to be hung in the lounge.
2) A pedestal and column in Dalbeatie granite bearing a suitable inscription and surmounted by a sundial.
3) Re-enforcing the surrounding and foundation of the rock garden.
4) Two ornamental garden seats to be placed either side of the memorial.
5) Two ornamental vases at the top of the steps leading to the memorial.
6) A brochure as a suitable memento of life occasion.

The memorial bears the inscription 'In memory of Isabel Cowe, who died at St Abbs Haven, January 3rd, 1931'. 'Erected by visitors'.

Unveiling of the Isabel Cowe Sundial Memorial at The Haven.

Unveiling of the Isabel Cowe Sundial Memorial at The Haven.

Memorial site and viewpoint

The Communion Table

A solid oak communion table with the inscription 'Sancta. Laneta. Sancta. Dedicated to the memory of Isabel Cowe, The Haven, Benefactress of St Abbs' was donated to Rev T. Donaldson Barr, of St Abbs Church of Scotland.

The communion table was used in the church until its closure. Fortunately, we still have the item which is being used in the exhibition of Isabel Cowe's life.

The Communion table

Miss Isabel Cowe – Pioneer

Throughout her life, Isabel Cowe pushed the boundaries of the conventional role a male-dominated society placed on women. She was a pioneer, in every aspect of her life, and like all pioneers, she challenged the conventions of her day.

'She felt in her soul the clear and unmistakeable conviction to disobey all and pursue her own way' that is the manner of the pioneer.

Miss Cowe fearlessly pursued her path of duty, and courageously put her convictions into practice. She set her sight on a vision of what she wanted for the future, and from this small fishing village on the Berwickshire coast, she paved the way as an independent business woman, setting an example to all men, women and children of the district and beyond.

This independence was not merely a matter of mind; it also involved physical changes in activity and dress. Activities such as cycling expanded women's ability to engage with a broader, more active world. In fact, it was said that 'the bicycle had done more to emancipate women than anything in the world.' It was seized by women as a tool of personal and political power, which was prevalent in these 'New Women' that emerged in the 1890s.

She taught us that the future lies with those who know their duty and who will follow it. The kings of men are not those who live upon or revive the old but those who can lead into the future.

Miss Cowe was a pioneer.

She was a woman of faith, and faith quite distinct from credulity of ignorant belief. She had faith in herself, in latent spiritual forces, in giant laws ever working in the spiritual world.

Miss Cowe had pioneering faith and expressed this through actions rather than words; she proved her faith by demonstration.

Coldingham Priory Graveyard

The Cowe family gravestone is located within the grounds of
Coldingham Priory.

The Cowe family gravestone, Coldingham Priory.

Eupemia Cowe, my great great grandmother & sister of Isabel Cowe.

Isabel Cowe, fishwives costume.

Isabel Cowe, fishwives costume.

Isabel Cowe, fishwives costume.

Northfield House, Laird Andrew Usher's residence

St Abbs Primary School. My great great grandfather, Alexander Gibson School-Master